WHAT CHRISTIANS BELIEVE

ABINGDON PRESS New York Nashville

WHAT CHRISTIANS BELIEVE

GEORGIA HARKNESS

WHAT CHRISTIANS BELIEVE

This book is printed on acid-free paper.

Library of Congress Catalog Card Number: 65-15232

ISBN: 978-1-5018-5389-0

17 18 19 20 21 22 23 24 25 26—10 9 8 7 6 5 4 3 2 1

MANUFACTURED IN THE UNITED STATES OF AMERICA

To lay Christians everywhere
who wish to understand their faith

CONTENTS

CHAPTER FOUR

CHAPTER FIVE

CHAPTER SIX

CHAPTER ONE

The Difference It Makes

Why is it important for Christians—or for anyone else—to know what Christians believe? Why is it not enough to live decently, treat other people fairly, and not bother about such questions? In short, if one is to be a Christian, why not just try to live by the Golden Rule and let it go at that?

The object of this first chapter is not to try to convince anyone that he ought to read this little book. That must be his own decision. But it is important to see that Christian belief is important. Perhaps this chapter can throw some light on the reasons why this is so.

Living with a due concern for others, which is the aim of the Golden Rule, is certainly a vital part of Christianity. Yet it is not the whole of it. Nor is this aim self-explanatory or self-generating, for where it is really vital it rests on deeper foundations.

Let us begin then with ground on which we all stand, and take a look at the social situation in the world today. Perhaps the most conspicuous thing about it is that we do not seem to have very firm ground to stand on! The evidences of change and unrest are all about us. The forms taken by this ferment vary from place to place, but there are few places that are untouched by the sources of change. The great technological advances, with the coming of automation and the nuclear space age; the advance of communism until it dominates one third of the world's population; the fear all over the world that the unleashing of atomic bombs may destroy us; the struggles of new nations in Asia and Africa toward self-government and nationhood; the stirrings of racial minorities in America and elsewhere in the demand for equality and justice; the awakening of underprivileged peoples in many lands to the need and the possibility of having food, freedom, and dignity—these and other forces have broken up the old moorings.

Some of this change is constructive in that it affords an incentive to the quest for better modes of living, and of living together. The social sciences have advanced along with the natural sciences, even though less conspicuously, and we understand more clearly than our fathers did the causes of physical and mental sickness, poverty, racial strife, alcoholism, narcotics addiction, and other social evils. Democracy advances, even though precariously and on uncertain foundations, in the newer nations. In spite of international tension there is more concern to find constructive alternatives to war than ever before. Even racial conflict—deplorable as it is when oppression stifles freedom or violence erupts—can be a spur to the concerned citizen to work for greater civil rights and a more just society.

Yet there are other aspects of the present situation which it is harder to view with any optimism. According to reliable reports from the FBI, which corroborate statistically what anyone can observe who reads the newspapers, crime is increasing rapidly. Such reports indicate that the increase in murder, aggravated assault, burglary, auto theft, and the like are nationwide in America and include all population groups. Add to these overt evidences of crime the growing frequency of broken homes, juvenile delinquency, premarital sex relations at the high school and college level, and widespread drinking at all ages, and it becomes apparent that our society is not in a healthy state.

This disease of society—write it as dis-ease and the term is equally appropriate—has no single cause. Yet underneath most of its symptoms lies a slipping of moral standards. And beneath this slipping lies "lostness," the lack of a sense of life's meaning and of ground to stand on to meet the inevitable problems that are bound at times to assail every soul.

In a rapidly changing world where the old securities are being broken up, inherited moral standards and values no longer seem as fixed or dependable as they once did. Then, unless there are reliable inner sources of guidance and support, the strain is too great for stable personal living. Multiply this a million fold, and an unstable society is the inevitable result.

It is at this point that personal uncertainty and social unrest converge. Tension is the order of the day, as is evidenced by enormous sales not only of alcoholic stimulants but also of tranquilizing drugs. The science of psychiatry is a genuine boon to which our fathers lacked access, but it may be doubted that there is an unmixed blessing in the present wholesale and expensive patronage of psychiatrists to assuage one's troubles. The suicide rate is alarming, and hosts of people live in anxiety, frustration, and dread of tomorrow.

This moral and spiritual unrest is worldwide. And it is intimately connected with religion, or the lack of it. In the Orient it is marked by a resurgence of the older religions, particularly Buddhism, Hinduism, and Islam, both as a means of filling in the vacuum and as a thrust against the Christianity thought to be too closely connected with the power structure of the West. In Europe and America the response is both an increasing secularization of society through the repudiation of Christianity and the rise of new movements for the renewal of the church.

It is religious faith which alone gives ultimate meaning to morality. This is by no means to say that all the decent people are religious! One may live to a ripe old age committing no crime, violating in no conspicuous way the accepted moral standards of a civilized culture, and yet not be a church member or committed Christian. This is true in spite of the significant fact that crime and social aberration are more common among those outside of churches than among those who attend church regularly. Yet a still more basic fact is also true—when faith is lost, much else that is precious goes with it. Provided one's religious faith is firm, yet flexible enough to view new conditions in the light of basic truth, this is the best corrective to slipping moral standards and uncertain personal values. Religious faith of the right kind nourishes insight and stamina, and both are immensely needed today.

This is one reason why stress is being laid in the churches on the importance of lay theology. It is an aspect of the recent trend toward the recognition of the laity as the church within the world, with emphasis on the recovery of a sense of the sacredness of the common life and "the priesthood of all believers." Yet even if the ecumenical movement had not inaugurated this emphasis on the mission of the laity, with the denominations accenting it, it would still be true that it is enormously important for all Christians to know what they believe.

To believe the wrong things can destroy one's life. To believe nothing can leave one floundering and catching at straws when stable support is needed. To believe only what has been inherited from the past encourages both a rigid inflexibility in one's own thought and an uncharitable dogmatism toward others who may think differently.

If one does not have a growing and vital religious faith to guide him, he will be guided in his attitudes and practice either by inherited ideas and prejudices or by current social pressures. Much is being said about the secularization of the churches. What this means, in effect, is that unless church members understand and consciously attempt to live by the implications of their faith, their attitudes and actions will be determined by those of the society around them. If they are not to live by community pressures and the persuasive forces that impinge on them constantly from business, politics, the television, or the newspaper, they must have a perspective from beyond these forces and agencies by which to judge them. Without a true and living faith there is a tendency, on the one hand, to become simply a social conformist and, on the other, to become a creature of impulse seeking self-expression, excitement, and pleasure in a sea of moral relativities.

Contrary to the assumption of some people, theology is not for the experts only; it is for everybody. There are aspects of it that require the most highly trained and penetrating scholarship. Yet in its elements it can be stated simply and in a way that is relevant to both personal and social living. There are theological abstractions, as there is also abstract science and abstract art. Exposed to these only, the person untrained in the field may throw up his hands in despair or make random guesses as to what it is all about. Yet, as science and art can be stated in simple enough terms to become meaningful and fascinating studies, so can theology. And, to carry the analogy further, as truly as science and art are indispensable aspects of human experience which both stem from and serve deep human needs, so religious truth is fundamental to life.

This small book is an attempt to say, as simply and briefly as possible, what Christians believe. At once the question arises, "Which Christians?" There are, of course, differences of belief among Christians. Not only are there many denominations, but there are deep lines of difference which cross denominational lines. These must be taken into account, and will be mentioned as the occasion seems to require it. Nevertheless, there are far more agreements than differences among Christians, and these agreements are far more important to human living than the differences. When Christianity is contrasted either with the other living religions of the world or with the secularism that threatens to engulf it in the West, the distinction is clear at vital points.

What these vital points are will be indicated by the chapter headings. We begin with belief in God, since this is the central pivot of any religious faith. In spite of the fact that "no one has ever seen God" (John 1:18), the belief in God persists in a science-oriented age, as it has in every previous age that has assailed it. If it could be presupposed that all readers were informed as to what is in the Bible and how best to find in it God's revelation of himself, we could then move directly to his supreme revelation in Jesus Christ. Since this assumption cannot be made, the third chapter deals with the Bible. In the fourth we focus on the centrality of Christ for Christian faith. The basic doctrines of the incarnation, the cross, and the resurrection are related to the historical events of the life and ministry of Jesus. In the fifth chapter we try to bring into meaningful synthesis the doctrine of the Trinity as Father, Son, and Holy Spirit; then move to the work of the Holy Spirit in creating and sustaining the Christian church. The final chapter on the Christian life deals with Christian salvation through the mastery of sin and pain and death by the goodness and power of God as he has come to us in Christ.

Readers who may be familiar with my previous writing on these subjects, and in particular my two earlier books of theology for laymen, *Understanding the Christian Faith*[1] and *Beliefs That Count*,[2] may wonder why another. The answer is that this is simpler, shorter, and less expensive than the others. I have not repeated the words of these other books, though naturally the ideas recur, since these are the things I most steadfastly believe. My hope is that this little book may lead to the reading of larger ones, not mine alone but the many good books along these lines by other authors.

Even more it is my hope and prayer that the reading and thinking on these themes may quicken Christian living. Without such response both the writing and the reading would be fruitless. *Knowing* must lead to *being* and to *doing*, or all three will tend to fade before the pressures of our time.

Let no one assume that the reading of this book, or of another, will make one a Christian, or put an end to the need for making difficult moral decisions. Being a Christian is a many-sided matter, of which knowing one's faith is but one aspect although

[1] (Nashville: Abingdon Press, 1947.)
[2] (Nashville: Abingdon Press, 1961.)

a very essential one. Being a church member, if this is to be more than a nominal relation, involves regular attendance for worship, fellowship with other Christians, material and moral support of the church as an organized body, service within the church and service as the church within the world. It calls for facing the problems of the day, whether of personal living or great social issues, with courage, insight, and the moral determination born of faith in God. Christianity is not a solitary religion or a private luxury. Its rewards both in inner peace of soul and outer conquest of evil are great, but the cost is heavy—the cost of giving one's entire life to God in trust, obedience, and service.

Thus, it should be kept in mind in reading this book that the term "Christian faith" has two very basic but related meanings. On the one hand, it means what Christians believe. This is primarily what this book is about. On the other, it means the Christian's commitment in trust to the God who has come to us in Jesus Christ, and an earnest attempt to live as a Christian in all of life's relationships. Christianity at its best does not choose between these two aspects of faith and center on one of them to the exclusion of the other; it unites the two.

Again and again this connection is presupposed in the Bible. It appears very clearly in the writings of Paul, the first great Christian theologian, whose practical injunctions to Christian living are not simply mingled with, but rest upon, the affirmations of Christian belief. Note, for example, his concern over those whose zeal outruns their knowledge: "Brethren, my heart's desire and prayer to God for them is that they may be saved. I bear them witness that they have a zeal for God, but it is not enlightened." (Rom. 10:1-2.)

In Paul's time, however, as in ours the main problem was apparently not excess of zeal but conformity to current worldly standards through lack of conviction and personal dedication. So, after eleven chapters of theology in the letter to the Romans, we find him bringing it all to a conclusion with these words:

I appeal to you therefore, brethren, by the mercies of God, to present your bodies as a living sacrifice, holy and acceptable to God, which is your spiritual worship. Do not be conformed to this world but be transformed by the renewal of your mind, that you may prove what is the will of God, what is good and acceptable and perfect. (Rom. 12:1-2.)

There, in a nutshell, is the reason why it is important to know what Christians believe. It is that "the renewal of your mind" may bear fruit in Christian living. Let us, then, read and think seriously about the foundations of our faith.

CHAPTER TWO

Belief in God

The basic foundation of a religion, whether Christianity or any other, is belief in God. Religions differ considerably as to how their adherents think of God, and from this primary difference many others follow. Yet in every religious faith there is belief in, trust and worship of, a Power believed to be more than man himself, and thus the object of man's ultimate concern.

This is sometimes disputed, for there are humanists who believe that a high regard for humanity is enough to constitute a religion. But is it? Without belief in God there can be a system of ethics, as in the social action for the improvement of human conditions in which humanists may engage without worshiping a deity. Without a deity there may also be forms of ritual and cultic practices, as in the initiation ceremonies of many secret societies and lodges. There may be a strong sense of devotion to a cause believed to be true and therefore bound to win, as in those who believe so strongly in the Communist ideology that they almost make of it a religious faith. Yet without belief in a deity believed to be more than man and more than the world of material things and economic forces—a deity so far above and beyond all else as to be worthy to be worshiped, trusted, and obeyed—there can be no religion in the true sense of the word.

In this chapter we shall be looking at what Christians in the mainstream of Christian faith believe about God. There are variations, to be sure, for Christianity through the centuries to the present has had many theological currents. Yet with all the changes that have come over Christian thought, there is a great unanimity of belief in the God of Christian faith.

But, first, how do we know what to believe about God?

1. *Sources of the knowledge of God.* An indispensable source of our knowledge of God is the Bible. This is why in the next chapter we must say something about how the Bible came to be written, and how best to interpret it to find in it the Word of God. In fact, the reader may go directly to that chapter now if he wishes. It has seemed wise to begin with God since he is the foundation of our faith, but we shall certainly understand better our relation to God if we understand the Bible. Probably an important reason why God seems so vague to many persons is that the Bible is even vaguer!

The whole Bible is a source of our knowledge of God, but it is not all on one level. What Christians find in the New Testament, and thus can see of God in the revelation that comes through Jesus Christ, is definitive for all the rest. In the ministry, teachings, death, and resurrection of Jesus Christians find their most dependable evidence of what God is like, though most Christians believe that our knowledge of God is not limited to what is expressly stated in the Bible by Jesus or about him. Not only what the Old Testament tells us in leading up to the coming of Jesus, but what has been discovered by Christian experience in the nearly twenty centuries since he lived, helps us to round out our knowledge.

Some of these convictions about God and his relation to men have been formulated by the church as creeds. Christians vary greatly as to how obligated they feel to accept the statements of these creeds as binding and authoritative. Some regard them as expressing complete and exact truth to which every real Christian must assent. Others regard the creeds of the church, like the Bible, as reflecting important angles of the truth which require interpretation rather than full assent in their literal form.

What comes to us through the Bible—and supremely through Christ in the New Testament—and then is handed down through being read, taught, and interpreted by Christians from generation to generation, is called biblical theology. Some Christians believe that this is the only dependable or important source of our knowledge of God. Others find evidences of God in the orderliness, the beauty, and the bounty of physical nature; in man's goodness, intelligence, and capacity for striving after the higher values of life; in the saints and seers of many faiths to whom the one God has revealed himself; in the religious experience of all mankind. This is called natural theology, or sometimes philosophical theology from its close connection with the philosophy of religion.

The prevalent type of theology among Christian scholars today is biblical theology, since it is to the Bible that one goes to find what is most distinctive about the Christian belief in God or Jesus Christ. However, a good many theologians, including the writer of this book, believe that if our knowledge of nature and of human experience is connected with that which comes through the Bible, it can be very useful as a supplementary source of our knowledge of the Creator. It can also be helpful as a bridge to a common world of experience outside the Christian church. For example, scientifically minded persons unfamiliar with the Bible can still feel a deep reverence before the Creator of the universe whose laws they seek to understand. The adherents of other faiths can find a common bond in reverence for the God who inspires the best aspirations of those who seek him through many forms of religious experience.

The point of view from which this book is written is that the revelation of God which comes to us in Jesus Christ and is known through the Bible is our firmest and truest foundation for the knowledge of God, but that this is not our only source. From this standpoint, let us look now at the main notes in the Christian understanding of God.

2. *God the Creator*. The Bible begins with the words, "In the

beginning God created the heavens and the earth" (Gen. 1:1). Many times afterward it is assumed that God is the Creator of all that exists. In the devotional poetry of the psalms it is affirmed that

> The heavens are telling the glory of God;
> and the firmament proclaims his handiwork (Ps. 19:1).

The prophet Isaiah encourages the fainthearted with the words,

> Have you not known? Have you not heard?
> The Lord is the everlasting God,
> the Creator of the ends of the earth.
> He does not faint or grow weary,
> his understanding is unsearchable (Isa. 40:28).

In the drama of Job, which wrestles with the problem of why the righteous must suffer, no philosophical explanation is given, but Job is made to feel his littleness before the almighty power of the Creator. (Job 38:1-42:6.)

In the words of Jesus found in the New Testament, he uses many references to the common things of nature, such as the birds of the air, the lilies of the field, the sun that rises on the evil and the good, and the rain that falls alike on the just and the unjust, in order to indicate the Creator's loving concern for all that he has made. (Matt. 5:45; 6:25-33.) In the parables of Jesus he uses such familiar scenes and events as a woman sweeping the house for a lost coin, a shepherd going out after a lost sheep, or a father welcoming home a lost boy, to suggest the yearning love of God. (Luke 15:3-32.) It never occurred to Jesus to doubt that God is the Creator of the entire world of man and nature.

Let us return to the creation stories in Genesis to see what they can tell us. The first chapter of Genesis was written quite late in the history of the Hebrews, after their return from exile in Babylon, while most of the second chapter is much earlier. Of the two the first chapter is the more beautiful and meaningful. But both these accounts of creation were written long before there was any science as we think of it today, and it is a great mistake to try to read them as if they were a scientific account of how the world came to be as it is. Yet in spite of this fact these ancient stories, particularly that with which the Bible opens, show very great spiritual insight, with truths suggested that can outlive any changes in scientific outlook.

Four truths of much importance stand out. These are: (1) that God is the one, only, and ultimate Creator of all that is; (2) that God has made man, both male and female, in his own spiritual image, and hence as a being of great dignity and worth; (3) that God has made us to "have dominion" over the rest of the created world—that is, to be his stewards and to hold what we have in trust to him; and (4) that in spite of all the evil we can see in the world, God's creation is good. Let us look briefly at each of these notes.

The Hebrews did not always believe that there is but one God. The earlier parts of Hebrew history reflect belief in henotheism rather than monotheism; that is, belief in the existence of the gods of other nations but worship of their own as supreme. Even the first of the Ten Commandments, "You shall have no other gods before me" (Exod. 20:3), probably reflects this period in their development. Yet by the time Isaiah wrote the passage quoted, the vision had become clear that there was and could be but one God, on whose holy will and creative power the whole universe depends. This was taken over into Christianity, and has remained there as very basic to the Christian understanding of God.

To say that "God created man in his own image" (Gen. 1:27) does not mean, of course, that God has a physical body such as we have. "God is spirit, and those who worship him must worship in spirit and truth," said Jesus. (John 4:24.) What it does mean is that God has created man as a morally responsible being, with freedom to choose between good and evil and the obligation to choose the good. It means that, finite and limited though we are, we still have capacities for love, goodness, wisdom, and creative power which are somewhat akin to those of

God. It means that God can have fellowship with us and we with him in a spiritual sense. Hence it means that God can speak to us to call us to obedience, to condemn us if we are unfaithful, to love us and draw us to himself. The infinite Creator, who is far above and beyond us all and ought to be worshiped in deep humility, has nevertheless so made us in his own spiritual image that we can feel him very near.

To say that God has set us in responsible stewardship over the rest of his created world is again to emphasize something important about both God and man. That God in the beginning created the heavens and the earth does not require us to believe that everything was finished, just as God would have it, at some far-off early point in time. The continued presence of God in his world, giving guidance and strength to his servants, suggests that creation continues. There is so much evil in the world that we cannot believe God desires everything to remain as it is. Instead, the thoughtful Christian believes that he has a responsibility given him by God to make the best possible use of his talents and material resources, and thus be God's servant in making this more nearly the kind of world God desires it to be.

This brings us to the most difficult of all problems of Christian faith—the problem of evil. There is no single or complete answer, but there are a number of important things that can be said about it. Among these are: (1) that evil in the form of human sin—the worst kind of evil—is caused by a misuse of the freedom of choice which God has given us for obeying his righteous will; (2) that much, though not all, of the world's suffering is caused by personal or social sin; (3) that natural evils, such as famines, floods, and earthquakes, occur within a natural order which God in his wisdom and goodness has given for us to live in, and he expects men to use their skills to "subdue the earth" for human good; and (4) that God has placed us in a great network of social relations, such as the family, the community, and the nation, in which we can greatly help but also greatly harm one another. He has placed upon us the responsibility of making these relations helpful, but through sin, ignorance, or plain indifference we often fail to do so, and evil inevitably results.

Some Christians believe in the existence of a personal devil, or Satan, as the source of evil. Others believe that such a dualistic idea is contrary to belief in the one good God as the Creator of all. Some believe that man's sinfulness is a curse inherited from Adam. Most Christian scholars view Adam as "man in general," which is what the word means, and find the source of sin in our own self-love and self-centeredness. The newer forms of depth psychology seem to reinforce this view.

In spite of the problems that arise about the cause of evil in God's good world, Christians believe that God stands ready to help us to conquer all forms of evil. Some can be eliminated, others triumphantly endured. What is required is that we love, obey, and trust him, and thus be enabled to confront what is evil without being crushed by it. This is stated many times in the Bible but perhaps most forcefully in the words of Paul, "We know that in everything God works for good with those who love him" (Rom. 8:28).

3. *Divine judgment.* We must turn to other basic notes in the Christian understanding of God. One of these was anticipated in suggesting that sin is the worst evil, always contrary to the will and purpose of a pure and holy God. Because all men are sinners, all stand under the divine judgment.

But what is sin? Though we must use the word frequently, it is not a simple, easy word to define. Christians usually think of it in two senses, either as a condition of one's total personality or as specific wrong acts or attitudes. In either case, it is something contrary to God's righteous and holy will.

As a state of the soul or selfhood, sin is described by some as being self-love and self-centeredness, by others as pride and self-righteousness, by still others as alienation or estrangement from the source of one's existence in God. These varying phases meet in the idea that man is a sinner because he persistently wants to have his own way and exalt himself instead of humbly submitting his life to the rule and loving care of God.

When sins are thought of as concrete evil acts, so numerous that they must be referred to in the plural, they are violations of the commandment to love God supremely and one's neighbor as one's self. The manifold forms they take are sometimes referred to as sins of omission (the failure to do what should be done) and sins of commission (positive acts of wrongdoing). Some of these are sins of the flesh through yielding too much to bodily impulses, but even harder to combat are evil tempers and dispositions. Such sins may or may not be condemned by the society around one, but what makes them sin is their being wrong in the sight of God.

Whether sin is viewed as a general state of the soul or as particular sins, Christians recognize that God cannot treat it lightly. There is austerity as well as love in the heart of God; he is no sentimental or indulgent parent of his great human family.

Divine judgment emphasizes the justice of the righteous God in his utter condemnation of sin, and hence his necessary punishment of the sinner who refuses to repent. This punishment often takes the form of the suffering that ensues within God's moral order when we break the laws of God and find ourselves broken as a consequence, as, for example, when we defy the laws of health or of harmonious social living. However, the biblical view of divine judgment goes deeper than this, even using the term "the wrath of God" to indicate that God will not be complacent before human sin. The Old Testament prophets repeatedly announced the doom of an unrighteous nation if it persisted in sin. The New Testament has this same note transferred to the individual, and made the more terrible by being thought of as judgment after death as well as in the present life.

Christians sometimes recoil from this thought of divine judgment as inconsistent with the love of God. However, the right way to interpret it is to keep God's love and God's justice together, each giving meaning and strength to the other. God is neither sentimentally indulgent nor vindictive. It is because God cares so much for man, his supreme creation made in his own image, that he is so grieved by man's sinning. The key to our understanding of divine judgment is God's yearning to save man from the sin that makes it necessary.

4. *God as Redeemer and Savior.* The heart of biblical faith lies in the conviction that divine judgment is never God's final word. It is the love and mercy of God which persist in spite of human sin that form the most distinctive note in Christianity.

A very dominant idea in the Old Testament is God's covenant with the Hebrews as his chosen people, whereby he promised to cherish, support, and defend them if they would be obedient to his will. They repeatedly sinned against him, both by going after "strange gods" and by falling into moral offenses against one another such as the prophets of social justice felt impelled to condemn. Yet God kept on loving his people and promising them a Redeemer, or Messiah, if even a remnant of them would respond to his call to obedience and trust.

Most of the people thought of this promised Messiah as a political deliverer who would restore the Jews to their former greatness as a nation. However, when Jesus came, he completely renounced this idea. As we shall see further in another chapter, Jesus thought of his mission as showing the love of God even for sinners and bringing people to new life through the love and mercy of God. What was required of them was faith, repentance, and humble obedience to the love commandment; then forgiveness and acceptance by God were assured.

It is in this message that Christianity took its rise. It was elaborated into a theology by the leaders of the church, especially by Paul; yet had not Jesus lived and taught this message, there would have been no Christianity. Because the followers of Jesus saw in him the incarnation of God himself, it became possible to speak of either God or Jesus as Lord and Savior, the Redeemer of sinful men. This does not mean that Jesus is a second God, for Christianity is a thoroughly monotheistic faith. It means that in Jesus Christians see the qualities of love, compassion, and mercy that lead them to repent of sin and give worship and obedience to the God whom he addressed as Father. As Paul expressed it, "God was in Christ reconciling the world to himself" (II Cor. 5:19).

5. *God as Father.* This brings us to the last of the terms by which Christians ordinarily speak of God. Here the word "father" is, of course, a symbolic term having no relation to biological parenthood; the term Creator serves better to indicate that God is the source of our being. However, Jesus taught his followers to pray to "our Father" and the Lord's Prayer, used by millions of Christians through the centuries and around the world, begins with the words,

> Our Father who art in heaven,
> Hallowed be thy name.

Since it was the word for God which Jesus used most often, it was adopted by the early church and has remained in the diction of Christians to the present. What it symbolizes is both simple and profound. As a heavenly Father God loves us, weak and sinful, erring or repentant, wise or foolish, as the case may be. Because he loves us, he turns none away. As in Jesus' parable of the prodigal son (Luke 15:11-32) we may be ever so unworthy of God's love and acceptance, but he loves us still. We have only to say with repentance and sincerity, "I will arise and go to my father," and we can be assured of the Father's forgiving welcome.

A derivative of this great thought about God is almost as important. Because God is the Father of all men, all men are brothers. If brothers, then we ought to treat one another as brothers, caring for and helping one another. There are some passages in the New Testament which suggest that we become sons of the Father and brothers of one another by becoming Christians, but Jesus' own vision seems to have been more inclusive than that. In one of his greatest parables about the requirements for a place in the kingdom of God he made the service to human need the basic condition. To those who were willing to help the hungry, the thirsty, the stranger, the naked, the sick and in prison, he represents the King as saying, "Truly, I say to you, as you did it to one of the least of these my brethren, you did it to me" (Matt. 25:31-46).

These four modes of thinking of God as Creator, righteous Judge, Redeemer, and Father are not all that could be said about the Christian understanding of God. Christians think of God as all-seeing, all-hearing, all-knowing, all-powerful, and eternal. He is the sovereign Ruler of the universe, the one God on whom our lives depend and from whom comes every good gift. Not only is he far above and beyond us in his infinity; he is also present with us and acting for us, always for good. He imparts comfort in our sorrows, light in our darkness, strength in our weakness. Thus the sovereign Ruler of the universe can be addressed in prayer, and the person who entrusts his life to God's keeping can feel his sustaining presence and from it gain new power for living.

This immediate presence and nearness of God Christians call the Holy Spirit. At this understanding of God as Holy Spirit we must look further in another chapter, after we have examined what Christians believe about Jesus. Yet it cannot be emphasized too strongly that Christians believe in the unity of the one true God. As Father he loves men with infinite compassion; in Jesus Christ we see him revealed most clearly; through the Holy Spirit we feel his presence, are guided by his wisdom, and sustained by his strength. Yet he is one God, never three, whom we find in our experience in these three major ways.

This conviction of Christians that we find the one God brought near and vital to us in three ways as Father, Son, and Holy Spirit is the doctrine of the Trinity. It is important, and we must certainly look further at it. What makes Christianity *Christian,* and not a branch of Jewish faith, is the centrality of Christ.

One is tempted therefore, to move directly to what Christians believe about Jesus. But are we ready? A look at the Bible was promised, and we shall understand Jesus better if we understand what is in the Bible and how best to weave together in our minds its many strands. To the Bible we now turn.

CHAPTER THREE

The Bible

It is unfortunate that to so many people the Bible is almost (or completely) unknown territory, for not only is it a basic source of knowledge for Christian faith but it has permeated deeply into the culture of the Western world and has laid the foundations for much of it. Biblical themes and quotations appear repeatedly in the masterpieces of literature, art, and music. They are found not only in the historic documents of the past but in great political utterances of our own time. It may be recalled that a very moving part of President Kennedy's funeral consisted of the reading of scripture passages that had been cited by him in his addresses. While present-day morality may be less specifically related to the Bible than was true in some former times, its roots are there in the biblical demand for responsibility before God, concern for one's neighbor, the worth of persons everywhere, and the need of liberty and justice for all. Not only does the Bible contain some of the world's greatest literature, but no other book has been nearly so influential throughout Europe and the Western hemisphere.

Since the Bible is a very large book—really a collection of sixty-six books—and this book is a very small one, it is possible to give only a brief survey of the contents of the Bible. However, this may be enough to give some idea of the variety and range of its literature and the nature of its message.

1. *Its general structure.* The Bible has many sources, and the history of how it came into existence has numerous strands. Much of the Bible, especially the Old Testament, was passed along by word of mouth for a long time before it was written down, and thus it is impossible to know who were the original authors. Even in the New Testament the four Gospels, which tell the story of the life, ministry, and teachings of Jesus, were compiled from what his followers remembered and from written fragments, and did not get put into their present form until some forty years after his death. Paul's letters to the newly formed churches are earlier than the Gospels, and it was the faith of the early church that prompted the compiling of the rest of the New Testament.

Christian scholars have done an enormous amount of research in regard to the various parts of the Bible. Some of this is *historical,* to determine as far as possible who wrote each book or section of it, when and where this occurred, and the circumstances, both religious and social, under which the writing was done. Other forms of research are *textual,* to determine the accuracy of the translations we have and of the background manuscripts from which these have been made. The results of these studies have given a better understanding of the Bible than was formerly possible, and a greater sense of the unity and integrity of the message of the Bible amid its various literary forms.

Furthermore, recent discoveries, both textual and archaeological, have tended to corroborate the Bible as it has come down to us. In 1947 the Dead Sea Scrolls were first found in a cave near the Dead Sea, with more and more discoveries since that date. Among the scrolls are parts of nearly every book in the Old Testament, the entire book of Isaiah, and a commentary on the book of Habakkuk which is rich in historical allusions. These are very early manuscripts, yet they differ only slightly and in unimportant details from the text which Christians have been using for centuries. Likewise in regard to the New Testament, in addition to the basic copies in Greek dating from the fourth century which are kept in the Vatican library at Rome and the British Museum in London, we have access to early translations into other languages such as Latin, Syriac, and Coptic, by which variations can be checked, and all are in essential agreement. Archaeological investigation goes on continually in and around various cities mentioned in the Bible, with the result that the historical events have in the main been corroborated.

With this knowledge, it need not disturb us to discover that most Christian scholars believe that the Bible developed by stages to its present form, and that therefore it reflects the attitudes of its authors and the conditions under which they wrote. Yet the message of the Bible is from God. Through the Bible God speaks, and has been speaking for many centuries, to inspire its readers to deeper faith and finer living. Hence the Bible is the Word of God regardless of some human imperfections in its words. Furthermore, in spite of its diversity of authors and social settings, the Bible in its central message of God's love for his people and his mercy and compassion even in their sinfulness has a remarkable unity.

2. *The Old Testament.* The Old Testament belongs to both Jews and Christians. The Jews regard this—but not the New Testament—as sacred Scriptures. Although to Christians the New Testament is the more basic, the Old Testament is also an essential part of the Christian Scriptures because it tells much about God and points toward the coming of Jesus as Messiah and Savior.

a. *The historical books.* In number of pages the largest section of the Old Testament consists of the books that trace the history of the Hebrew people. Let us review this rapidly.

The Bible begins with the story of creation, of which two accounts are given. Almost immediately comes the story of Adam's disobedience to God's command and hence the entrance of sin into God's good world. For this Adam and Eve are driven out of the Garden of Eden. Their sons Cain and Abel quarrel and Cain kills Abel. The sinning of Adam's and Eve's descendants continues until God sends a great flood which engulfs all the people except Noah and his family, and the population must start over again. Yet this does not eliminate sin, for strife and selfish pride lead to building a tower of Babel to try to reach up to heaven. After this there are so many languages the people do not understand one another.

Are these stories history or legend? Christians differ on this question, but many scholars believe their truth lies in what they reflect about human nature rather than in their historical accuracy. The word "Adam" comes from the Hebrew word that means "man," and his temptations are those of every man.

Then comes the period of the patriarchs. Abraham, convinced that the Lord was leading him, went out from Ur, near the Persian Gulf, and traveled westward to Canaan, which was later to be called Palestine. He was assured by God that God would make him the father of a great nation. Abraham's wife Sarah bore him a son in her old age who was named Isaac.

A dramatic part of the story is Abraham's willingness to offer his son Isaac in human sacrifice until God stayed his hand. In the next generation Isaac and his wife Rebecca had twin sons, Jacob and Esau. Through Esau's trickery the birthright was passed on through Jacob, so that the Jews often speak of Abraham, Isaac, and Jacob as their spiritual as well as biological ancestors.

Jacob had twelve sons, from whom the twelve tribes of the Hebrew people were later to be named. One of these, Joseph, was so disliked by his brothers that they threw him into a pit from which he was rescued by a caravan and taken to Egypt. He there arose to power, and when a famine occurred in Canaan and his brothers came to Egypt seeking grain, though they did not recognize him, he was able as the pharaoh's steward to provide them with it. They and their families then moved to Egypt. All of these stories are told with great vividness and fascinating detail. They doubtless have a foundation in fact although they reveal also the storyteller's art.

The spotlight now shifts to the slavery and oppression of the Hebrews in Egypt and their miraculous deliverance by God as Moses led them out of bondage. Moses was a Jew who had been brought up at court by the ruling pharaoh's daughter, but who decided to cast his lot with his own people. The Exodus, as their escape from Egypt was called, was ever after to bulk large in Jewish thought, and is to the present the basis of their Passover observance.

For many years the people were nomads in what is now called the Sinai peninsula. The climax of this period is Moses' receiving the Ten Commandments from God on Mount Sinai, where God's covenant with Abraham was renewed. The covenant, which was to remain basic throughout the Old Testament, was God's promise to guide and deliver the Hebrews as his chosen people if they in turn would obey him. The New Testament (which means the "new covenant") later broadens this relation to include all mankind.

There is no doubt that Moses lived and that he was a very great man. He took what had been a band of downtrodden serfs in Egypt and by God's help he pulled them together into a nation with a great sense of their destiny and of the sacredness of their relation to God. The Ten Commandments provide a set of moral standards which are still vital to both Jewish and Christian thought.

Moses did not live to enter Canaan. Joshua took over the leadership of the people, and after a considerable struggle the land was conquered. For quite a long time, called the period of "the Judges," there was strife and anarchy under local warlords. A more stable and unified rule was needed; first under Saul, then later under the great King David, the land was united to become one kingdom. In all of these events the Hebrews believed that the hand of the Lord was leading them.

The united kingdom lasted through the reign of David's son Solomon; then fell apart into two sections which are usually referred to as the Northern and Southern Kingdoms. There was rivalry between these groups as well as constant danger and frequent attacks from the Assyrians and Babylonians to the east and Egypt in the southwest. Palestine, then as now, was a buffer state lying between great powers, and its location made it open to conflict and dissension. In 721 B.C. the Northern Kingdom, with its capital at Samaria, fell to the Assyrians and was never restored. The Southern Kingdom, centered at Jerusalem, was conquered by the Babylonians in 586 and the most virile of its people were carried into exile. There they learned that they could worship God even away from their homeland, and as we shall see presently, some of their greatest religious insights came out of this experience.

Let us stop now and take a look at how these events became recorded. This may be a bit confusing because what stands first in the Bible was not written first. The earliest contemporary writing of history is found in the stories of the prophet Samuel and of the kings Saul and David about 1000 B.C. David had a court recorder, and it is probable that these accounts were taken from records made as the events were happening. They form a direct, very realistic-sounding narrative largely free from miraculous incidents.

The first five books of the Bible, called the Pentateuch, and most of Joshua and Judges were written later, in four stages. About 850 B.C. and again about 750 B.C. two writers with a marvelous gift for storytelling either wrote or compiled the remembered history of their people. Since we do not know their names, they are referred to as "J" and "E" from the names they used for God. In 621, as the temple was being repaired, the book of Deuteronomy, or "D," was found. After the exile, when priestly influence prevailed, another writing was produced which contained a rather extended law code and also the beautiful story of creation which is the first chapter of Genesis. From its priestly source this is called "P." Some unknown editor or editors wove the four strands together to make one connected story, much as we now have it.

To return to the sequence of events as they occurred, Cyrus the King of Persia conquered Babylon while the Jews were in exile, and he permitted them to return to their homeland in 538. The story of these postexilic years is told in the books of Ezra and Nehemiah, though the greatest writing of this period is devotional and philosophical poetry. But before this came the prophets.

b. *The prophets.* The "high-water mark" of the whole Old Testament, with the possible exception of the devotional poetry of the Psalms, is found in the ethical and spiritual utterances of the prophets. Those whom Christian scholars usually consider to have been major prophets are Amos, Hosea, Isaiah, Micah, Jeremiah, Ezekiel, and the Second Isaiah.

Amos was the first of these to write his message down, about 750 B.C., and the book of Amos is the earliest complete book in the Bible. He proclaimed God's concern for social justice in resounding terms, and announced that doom would fall upon a nation that disobeyed God by defrauding and exploiting one's fellow men.

Hosea, suffering from his wife's faithlessness but still loving her, tells of God's yearning love for his people even when they sin. His note is more tender than that of Amos, stressing love where Amos put the emphasis on justice.

The first Isaiah, for apparently there were two prophets of this name living about 150 years apart, combined the messages of the justice and mercy of God. He was a statesman of keen political as well as spiritual wisdom, who warned the people to trust in God rather than in deceptive alliances with either Egypt or Assyria. However, his greatest contribution was the beginning of the messianic hope of a Redeemer and Deliverer to be sent by God—a hope which sustained the Jews through many dark days.

Micah was less creative than his three predecessors. However, he had the insight to restate Isaiah's vision, as yet unfulfilled, of a world without war in which men should beat their swords into plowshares and their spears into pruning hooks. A word of Micah's which is often quoted by both Jews and Christians as summing up the demands of the religious life is this: "He hath shewed thee, O man, what is good; and what doth the Lord require of thee, but to do justly, and to love mercy, and to walk humbly with thy God?" (Mic. 6:8 KJV.)

Jeremiah was one of the greatest of the prophets. Misunderstood and persecuted, he nevertheless continued to proclaim the voice of the Lord as he heard it. He believed it was futile for the Jews to resist the powerful conquerors from the east, yet beyond the fall of Jerusalem he foresaw a time when God would make a new covenant, written in the hearts of men. Then all should know God, from the least to the greatest, and he would forgive their iniquity and remember their sin no more.

Ezekiel, speaking to the Jews during their time of exile, proclaimed the majesty and holiness of God and helped the Jews to keep up their faith and courage through trust in God. His message abounds in visions and symbols, of which one of the most dramatic is the valley of dry bones receiving new life through the Spirit of God. (Ezek. 37:1-14.)

Second Isaiah was the greatest prophet of them all. In great poetic passages he sings of a coming Redeemer and of the mission of the Jews to be the suffering servants of God, and thus to carry the message of the love of God to all people. He declared unequivocally that there is but one God, the Creator of all that is, condemned idolatry, and called upon the people to submit to God in obedience and trust.

c. *Hebrew poetry.* Some of the Bible's greatest messages were spoken in poetry. There was poetry in the writings of the prophets, but the Bible has other types also. Since Hebrew poetry is marked by balance of thought and arrangement of ideas rather than rhyme and meter, the line between prose and poetry is sometimes indistinct, but there is unquestionably beautiful, moving poetry in the Old Testament.

Some of the earliest fragments of the Old Testament, inserted in the historical narrative, consist of patriotic songs which urge the warriors to battle or celebrate their victories. There are also several complete books of poetry. The book of Job is not only poetry but philosophy. It is a sort of drama which wrestles with the eternal problem of why the righteous must suffer in God's good world. The book of Psalms is a collection of hymns written over many centuries, probably some but not all of them by King David. They are greatly loved by both Jews and Christians because they express so vividly the aspirations of the human heart and the strength to be found in the goodness and greatness of God. The book of Proverbs is a collection of adages, full of shrewd and sensible wisdom. Ecclesiastes shows the influence of Greek hedonistic philosophy, and therefore must have been written late in Jewish history after the Jews came in contact with it. The Song of Solomon has as its theme romantic love, and probably consists of a collection of songs sung at weddings.

Here we must stop with our survey of the Old Testament, though it contains other books such as the charming story of Ruth, the stirring account of Queen Esther's intervention with King Ahasuerus to save her people, and the prophet Jonah's interrupted but effective missionary journey. Enough has been said to indicate the great variety of types of literature in the Old Testament, and the wide range of personalities and social settings reflected both in its writers and those written about. Yet everywhere God is lifted up as the Creator, Ruler, and righteous Judge of all men; and in its highest passages the love and the mercy of God even for his sinning and erring people become unmistakably clear.

3. *The New Testament.* The structure of the New Testament is very much simpler than that of the Old Testament. Not only is it much shorter, but it contains only three main types of literature. These are: (1) the four Gospels and the book of Acts, which are mainly narrative accounts of events interspersed with conversation and sermons; (2) the letters of Paul and some others, addressed to the churches; (3) the book of Revelation, which is a special kind of literature called apocalyptic.

a. *The letters.* The four Gospels and the book of Acts stand first in the New Testament but, as we saw to be true of the Old Testament, what now stands first was not the first to be written.

Paul, a Jew of the strict sect of the Pharisees who were much devoted to the Jewish law and were its official interpreters, at first violently persecuted the Christians. But a few years after Jesus' crucifixion he became converted through a dramatic experience on the Damascus road, and after that he was a great leader and champion of Christianity. He was a theologian, preacher, counselor, missionary evangelist, and administrator all in one. As he traveled from place to place, preaching the gospel of the new Christian faith, he founded numerous churches. Then he kept in touch with them, revisiting them sometimes but also writing letters to encourage and admonish them. Enough of these letters were saved so that they form the earliest part of the New Testament writing. Christians still find them very valuable, both for their universal message to every age and for what they disclose about the faith and activities of Christians when the church was new.

There are nine of these letters which bear the names of the churches to which Paul addressed them. These are Romans, I and II Corinthians, Galatians, Ephesians, Philippians, Colossians, I and II Thessalonians. Another very personal letter, Philemon, was addressed to an individual by this name as Paul sent a runaway slave back to his master with tender words of commendation. There are three other personal letters, I and II Timothy and Titus, which bear Paul's name but may have been written by Christians later, since they reflect a later stage in the development of the church.

In addition to these letters of Paul or those attributed to him, there are eight more letters in the New Testament which it is certain Paul did not write. These are Hebrews, James, I and II Peter, I, and II, and III John, and Jude. Thus, of the twenty-seven books of the New Testament, twenty-one are messages of fellowship to other Christians in particular situations. They vary in interest and value, but in every case there is a message which at vital points still touches our lives today.

b. *The Gospels and Acts.* We can look at the four Gospels and the book of Acts together because Acts was written by the same man who wrote the third Gospel, Luke, and originally it was probably all one book. It became separated in order to place together the four accounts of Jesus' life and ministry.

The Gospels deal mainly with the events of Jesus' public ministry, his teaching and healing, his crucifixion and resurrection. After the accounts of his birth given in Matthew and Luke and the one incident of his going with his parents to the temple at Jerusalem when he was twelve, we learn no more about him until he began his ministry. This was inaugurated by his being baptized by his cousin John the Baptist in the river Jordan when he was about thirty. We wish the writers of the Gospels, who are often called the four Evangelists, had told us more about the early life of Jesus, but they recorded only what seemed to them the most important. That they thought the crucifixion and resurrection the most important of all is evidenced by the fact that they gave fully one fourth of the entire account to the events of Jesus' last week on earth.

Of the four Gospels Mark is the earliest, having been written about A.D. 70 or a little before that. Mark's account plunges directly into the events of Jesus' baptism and ministry, with no reference to his birth or parentage. Matthew was written next, and in this account the author apparently used both Mark's story of Jesus' ministry and a collection of the sayings of Jesus, now lost except as Matthew arranged them systematically and placed them at intervals within the narrative. Luke, the third Gospel to be written, drew from the same sources but did not select exactly the same items, so that some parts are duplications while others are not. Luke shows the human, compassionate side of Jesus more clearly than the others. In this account we find some of Jesus' greatest parables, such as the story of the good Samaritan who serves one of another race in neighborly love and the prodigal son who is welcomed home joyously by his loving father when he does not deserve to be thus received.

The first three Gospels, though they differ somewhat, are much alike and for this reason they are called the "Synoptic Gospels," which means "seeing with one view." The fourth

Gospel, John, is generally believed to have been written considerably later, toward the end of the first century A.D., and thus it reflects more than the others do what the faith of the early church had come to be. Yet all of the Gospels do this to some degree. Instead of saying that we have a biography of Jesus, or an exact record of his teaching, it is more correct to say that we have the portrait of Jesus as the church thought of him—a picture accurate enough for Christians to see in Jesus the revelation of God, yet interpreted through the eyes of those who knew, remembered, and loved him.

The book of Acts is the story of the birth of the Christian church. Almost at the beginning is the account of Pentecost, when the Spirit of God, which was thereafter to be called the Holy Spirit, came upon the assembled disciples to give them great zeal and strength. The book then tells many incidents of their preaching and witnessing as they struggled against great obstacles. These incidents include the conversion and work of Paul, and something of the problems that had to be met when Gentiles as well as Jews embraced the new faith. Acts ends with Paul's being taken as a prisoner to Rome, where he was probably put to death, although the story ends abruptly with his being there in his own rented house and preaching quite openly. The book of Acts as a whole is a very vivid account of how Christ's early followers put their faith into works.

c. *Apocalypse*. The word "apocalypse" means "vision." The last book of the Bible, called the Revelation of Saint John, grew out of the time of severe persecution which the Christians had to endure toward the end of the first century. When it was not possible to defend the faith openly, its author used much cryptic symbolism to convey a message of hope and courage to those suffering for their faith. It is a book which many Christians find hard to understand, but through it breathes the hope of better days to come on earth, and beyond these, eternal life in the presence of God. Its keynote is, "The Lord reigneth."

4. *The Bible as the Word of God*. It is apparent from even this brief survey of how the various parts of the Bible came to be

written that it cannot be said to have been spoken directly by God and taken down with infallible accuracy by the persons who wrote it. Some Christians believe it to have been thus verbally inspired, and these persons feel that such a historical and literary study as we have just summarized takes away from the Bible any claim to divine inspiration. That this does not necessarily happen is evidenced by the fact that great numbers of Christians, including nearly all biblical scholars, still believe that the Bible is our chief source of knowledge of God and of what he gives to and demands of men. The Bible is God's Word if he speaks to us through it, as Christians believe that he most certainly does. It is not a mechanical speaking, like a phonograph record, but a living, vital medium by which God speaks today to those who will listen to him. It is through the Bible, read in the faith that is not credulity but openness of mind and heart, that we best learn of God and of what he has done and is still doing for men. Thus the real inspiration of the Bible lies in this Word, not in the words which bear the marks of human frailty.

Christians call the Bible the Holy Bible. This is not because it has no imperfections, but because even in spite of them the holiness of God shines through it.

In the Old Testament we see God leading the Hebrew people forward, and through their prophets and seers implanting a great hope of a coming Messiah who would be their Redeemer and Savior. In the New Testament we see how this hope was fulfilled in the coming of Jesus, who through his teaching and ministry, his death and resurrection, brought into the world from God a new source of light and the transformation of life through the gospel, or good news, of salvation.

But how did this happen? Why did this Galilean carpenter become the most influential figure in all history? At this question we must look in the next chapter.

CHAPTER FOUR

Jesus Christ

We come now to what is most distinctive in Christianity. This is the belief in, and devotion to, Jesus—usually referred to as Jesus Christ. The word Christ is not a surname, but a title which comes from the Greek word meaning "the anointed one." Its use from the first century onward, giving rise to the word "Christianity," indicates that Christians have always seen in Jesus a special revelation of God. No one doubts that Jesus was a man, but Christians see in Jesus something more than a religious genius, a prophet, or a saint. Christians believe that through Jesus as the incarnation of God it is possible to know the nature and reality of God, and to feel the power of God for salvation and moral direction in a way that is not possible through any other man. In a word, Christians believe that Jesus was both human and divine.

In spite of some variations among Christians as to how to think of Jesus, there has been a central core of agreement through the centuries. It is this that we shall now consider.

1. *The historical facts.* All Christians agree that Jesus was a Jew who was born in Palestine—which was then a province of the Roman Empire—during the reign of King Herod as the local

monarch and of Caesar Augustus at Rome. The Christian era dates our calendars from the reputed year of his birth, but since Herod died in 4 B.C. it is probable that Jesus was born a little before that time. He was born in Bethlehem, a small village south of Jerusalem traditionally associated with the name of King David, from whom Jesus was believed to be a descendant.

Accounts of Jesus' birth are given in two of the Gospels, Matthew and Luke. This is one of the points at which there is a difference of opinion among Christians, for some regard these birth stories as factual history, others as beautiful poetic legends which convey symbolically great meaning. Both the Matthew and Luke accounts suggest, though there is no further reference to it in the Bible, that Mary the mother of Jesus was a virgin, and thus that he was miraculously conceived. According to Matthew, Joseph's reluctance to take Mary as his wife was overcome by reassurance from an angelic messenger. Jesus' birth was heralded by a star which brought wise men from the east to do homage and to lay before him gifts of gold, frankincense, and myrrh. Warned in a dream that Herod sought the young child's life, Joseph then took Mary and Jesus and fled to Egypt. Later they returned to Nazareth in Galilee, where the child grew up.

According to Luke's account, Joseph and Mary were living in Nazareth when summoned to Bethlehem by an imperial census, whereupon Jesus was born in a stable because there was no room in the inn. Shepherds watching their flocks by night were startled by a celestial light as the glory of the Lord shone around them; whereupon an angel reassured them and an angelic chorus sang,

> Glory to God in the highest,
> and on earth peace among men
> with whom he is pleased! (Luke 2:14.)

The shepherds then went to Bethlehem, found Mary and Joseph with the babe lying in a manger, and told the wondrous things they had seen and heard. The shepherds returned, glorifying and praising God, while "Mary kept all these things, pondering them in her heart" (Luke 2:19).

What shall we do with these stories? They have become familiar throughout the Christian world through carols, pageants, and other Christmas observances. They cannot be disregarded. But neither must they be taken as literal history to find great meaning in them. Christians are divided on this question, but even those who feel no obligation to believe in a miraculous birth still believe in the centrality and uniqueness of Jesus. On this there is full agreement.

We know nothing of Jesus' childhood as he grew up in Nazareth in the home of Joseph the carpenter, being generally regarded by the townspeople as Joseph's son, except for one incident of a trip to Jerusalem with his parents at the age of twelve. Fascinated by what he heard in the temple, the boy lingered when the company started back and became separated from his family. At the conclusion of this story, in which Joseph and Mary are repeatedly referred to as his father and mother, we find one inclusive descriptive sentence, "And Jesus increased in wisdom and in stature, and in favor with God and man" (Luke 2:52). It may be inferred that he grew up as a thoughtful, eager-minded Jewish boy, learning of the wisdom of his ancestors in the synagogue school, working with Joseph in the carpenter shop, and after Joseph's death becoming the mainstay of the home in the support of Mary and his younger brothers and sisters.

About the age of thirty, Jesus apparently believed that God had called him, and that the time had come, to launch out upon a larger mission. Leaving his home in Nazareth he went to the river Jordan, where his cousin John the Baptist was already preaching divine judgment with a stern call to repentance, and received baptism. Thereupon he withdrew to the wilderness for an extended period of fasting and prayer. During this time of soul-searching in which he was apparently trying to discover the will of God for his life, he underwent three temptations which are graphically described by both Matthew and

Luke as temptings of the devil. These temptations—to command the stone to become bread, to leap from the temple pinnacle to demonstrate that God would save him, and to bow down and worship Satan in order to receive power over all the kingdoms of the world—may be taken as symbolic indications of his temptation to use his God-given powers for self-centered and ungodly ends. Some scholars believe that he already thought of himself as the expected Messiah and was trying to determine the nature of his leadership of his people.

When Jesus returned to Nazareth his mind was apparently made up. He took as his goal the words of Second Isaiah:

> The Spirit of the Lord is upon me,
> because he has anointed me to preach good news to the poor.
> He has sent me to proclaim release to the captives
> and recovering of sight to the blind,
> to set at liberty those who are oppressed,
> to proclaim the acceptable year of the Lord. (Isa. 61:1-2; Luke 4:18-19.)

From that time on he went about as an itinerant preacher, teaching and healing and using his powers completely in the service of God and the people, calling people to repentance for their sins, forgiving the penitent, imparting new life to many.

The dominant note in both the message and the life of Jesus was love to God and love to one's fellow man—a love made possible by the prior love of God the Father of all mankind for all his children. Because Jesus believed all men, including sinners and outcasts, to be precious to God, he did not hesitate to mingle with them, thereby shocking those who prided themselves on their own virtue. Because he thought that the official interpreters of the law, the Pharisees, were too legalistic and even hypocritical, he did not hesitate to rebuke them sharply. At the same time he set forth in pungent sayings what it would really be like to love and trust God and "seek first his kingdom and his righteousness" (Matt. 6:33).

His central message of the kingdom of God was usually proclaimed in parables which, through a simple story or example familiar to his hearers, carried a deep meaning. In this way he called men to accept the righteous rule of God in their lives and treat one another as brothers. Among the greatest of Jesus' parables is that of the prodigal son, which illustrates the forgiving love of God even for an erring and ungrateful son (Luke 15:11-32), and the good Samaritan, which shows that true neighborliness crosses racial, national, and religious lines to help another in need (Luke 10:29-37). To guard against discouragement when the kingdom seems to come very slowly because of the evil in the world he told the parable of the sower, whose planting is devoured by the birds or withered by the sun on rocky, shallow soil or choked by thorns, while some of the seed falls on good ground and brings forth abundantly. (Matt. 13:1-23.)

Wherever Jesus went, he had great compassion upon the sick and suffering people, and he used the powers God gave him to help them. Many in the diction of that day were believed to have "evil spirits," which we should now probably call forms of neurosis or insanity, and Jesus drove out their "demons" and restored them to sanity. By some power which we do not fully understand and need not hesitate to call miraculous, he healed many forms of illness.

Even more serious than bodily or mental illness was the sickness of men's souls through the many forms of sin to which human nature is subject. Wherever he went he brought strength to the weak, courage to the anxious, forgiveness to the repentant sinner, and set men and women on the way to better and stronger living through the power of God in their lives. So, not only did he talk about the love of God, but he demonstrated it in his own living. He practiced what he preached.

Toward the beginning of his ministry Jesus chose twelve men as his disciples to travel about with him and to learn from him. Among them the closest to him were Peter, James, and John. None of the disciples understood him fully and one of them, Judas, was later to betray him to his death for thirty pieces of silver. Yet this nucleus was destined to carry on the work of Jesus after his death and resurrection, and hence the disciples are of great importance to the subsequent birth of the church. On one occasion Jesus asked them, "Who do you say that I am?" and Peter answered, "You are the Christ, the Son of the living God" (Matt. 16:15, 16). For this insight Jesus commended him, and the Roman Catholic Church believes that this gave Peter a special commission to become later the head of the church.

The ministry of Jesus lasted somewhere between one and three years—we do not know exactly. Then opposition arose from the Pharisees who were the custodians of the law, from the Sadducees who were a wealthy and aristocratic priestly class in charge of the temple, from the Roman rulers who feared for their own power in this new popular movement, and from the Jews who had looked to Jesus to throw off the Roman yoke and were disappointed that he did nothing of this kind.

The Gospels tell vividly of Jesus' triumphal entry into Jerusalem on what is now observed as Palm Sunday, with the crowds waving palm branches to honor him. Yet before the week was over they were shouting, "Crucify him." Into the events of that tragic last week are packed the stories of his cleansing of the temple from its commercialism—thus outraging the money changers, the last supper as Jesus ate the Passover meal with his disciples and told them of his impending death, the betrayal by Judas, Jesus' agony in the Garden of Gethsemane as he shrank from death but accepted it as God's will, the mockery of a trial before the Jewish leaders, the Roman governor Pontius Pilate's vacillation and surrender to the people's demand for his death. On Friday of that week, Jesus was crucified between two thieves.

Yet this is not the end of the story. Christians believe that on the third day Jesus rose again from the dead, thus demonstrating the victory of God and the power of God over human sin and bodily death. As the suffering of Jesus on the cross is commemorated throughout the Christian world every Good Friday—a very dark Friday made good through the self-giving love of

God—so the joy of resurrection is celebrated on Easter morning. The resurrection is vital to Christian faith, for it means the presence of the living Christ among his followers. Furthermore, it brings the promise of eternal life through the goodness and power of the same God who brought Jesus from the dead.

The death of Jesus on the cross is a plain historical fact. About the resurrection there is more uncertainty as to exactly what happened. The Gospel accounts all agree that it did happen, and the church came into existence in the faith that it had happened. In the assurance of the living presence of their Lord, a disheartened little band of disciples became flaming witnesses for Christ. Yet the Bible gives no clear picture of its nature. Christians continue to interpret it in various ways, sometimes as a physical miracle, sometimes as a spiritual presence, sometimes as a foregleam of the "spiritual body" which Paul says God will give us after death (I Cor. 15:35-44).

In any case the resurrection is a miracle in the sense of something wonderful that occurred by the power of God. The important thing is not to get an exact description of it, but to discover its meaning for human life. Because of this meaning, Easter is one of the greatest days in the Christian year, celebrated by serious-minded Christians with a holy joy.

We have looked at the principal events in the brief earthly life of Jesus. We must now consider why Christians regard him not only as Teacher and Master but as Lord and Savior.

2. *The incarnation.* The word "incarnation" means "in the flesh." It is used in Christian theology to designate the belief that, as the first chapter of the Gospel of John puts it, "The Word became flesh and dwelt among us, full of grace and truth; we have beheld his glory, glory as of the only Son from the Father" (John 1:14). This emphasizes the revelation of God in Jesus, whereby in beholding the kind of man he was and seeing how much of the will and purpose of God are reflected in his ministry, we can more clearly discern the nature of the God he worshiped and taught men to love and to serve.

The theology of the incarnation is sometimes considered under the headings of the "person" and the "work" of Christ. As the passage just quoted describes his personality as Son in relation to God as Father, other passages of the Bible speak of what Christ has done for mankind in bringing to sinful men the forgiving love and saving grace of God by which to lead a new life. One of the great passages often quoted in this connection is from the words of Paul:

> Therefore, if any one is in Christ, he is a new creation; the old has passed away, behold, the new has come. All this is from God, who through Christ reconciled us to himself and gave us the ministry of reconciliation; that is, God was in Christ reconciling the world to himself, not counting their trespasses against them, and entrusting to us the message of reconciliation. (II Cor. 5:17-19.)

When Jesus Christ is thought of in this connection, he is not only the revealer of God but the Redeemer of men.

Note that the New Testament almost always speaks of Jesus as the *Son* of God. The most authentic biblical position does not equate him with the one God whom he himself trusted and served and to whom he prayed. Rather, it expresses his uniqueness as the supreme channel by which men may come to know this one true God, and through trust in the love of God as he comes to us through Christ can be delivered from the bondage of sin and pain and death.

Christians who believe in the virgin birth of Jesus, as Roman Catholics, the Eastern Orthodox, and a great many Protestants do, usually consider it essential that the Son of God should have been miraculously born. There are others, however, who believe equally in the divinity of Jesus as the Son of God but find their assurance of it in himself regardless of his birth. When one considers what Jesus was and what he did for the lives of persons in his earthly life, and then what as the risen Lord and the Christ of faith he has been doing for his followers in all the centuries since, it is *all* a miracle which gives clear evidence of his divinity.

We have noted that his earthly name was Jesus but that he is now spoken of as Christ or as Jesus Christ. This is no accident, for it was mainly after the resurrection that he came to be called Christ. His followers called him this when through faith they saw in him "the anointed one" of God, the expected Messiah, but more than that, the Lord and Savior of all men who would find God through him. Thus, the use of the name Christ is closely linked with both the incarnation and the resurrection, though Christians do not always recognize this fact.

3. *The meaning of the cross.* The cross is the central symbol of the Christian faith. But why? The death of Jesus at the hands of evil men who misunderstood and hated him is a historical fact, but is this enough to account for its centrality?

The Christian doctrine of the cross is traditionally called the doctrine of the atonement, which literally means at-one-ment. This suggests that in a vital way the death of Jesus bridged the gap between men and God and brought about a closer unity.

This must not be taken to mean that God had ever cut himself off from men, or stopped loving them even when they were sinners. On the contrary, it is *men* who separate themselves from God by indifference, disobedience, and sometimes outright rebellion. God keeps on loving us through everything, and when we cannot by our own effort save ourselves, because of forgetfulness of him, he wins us back through love and offers new life in Christ. This lies at the heart of Christian faith and experience, and Paul has said it for us in the words, "God was in Christ reconciling the world to himself, not counting their trespasses against them" (II Cor. 5:19). To these we may add others which speak specifically of Christ's death: "While we were yet helpless, at the right time Christ died for the ungodly. Why, one will hardly die for a righteous man—though perhaps for a good man one will dare even to die. But God shows his love for us in that while we were yet sinners Christ died for us." (Rom. 5:6-8.)

The death of Jesus must be thought of in close relation to what came before and after it. In his total ministry God was speaking through his Son and drawing men away from sin to salvation. In Jesus' obedience even to death and in the resurrection which followed, God's love and mercy and God's power over sin and death become unmistakably clear.

In the cross Christians find both the *pattern* of the way we ought to live and the *power* from God to lead better and stronger lives. Suffering love is at the heart of it. Humble about our own goodness or achievement, we must be grateful to God that in Christ we find the love of God for our forgiveness and strengthening. As doctrines of the cross have tried in various ways to say, Jesus died for us. Christ died for our redemption.

This is a mystery, as the mighty acts of God always are. Long before the time of Christ, Second Isaiah spoke words of wisdom which apply to this, as to much else in the ways of God:

> For my thoughts are not your thoughts,
> neither are your ways my ways, says the Lord.
> For as the heavens are higher than the earth,
> so are my ways higher than your ways
> and my thoughts than your thoughts. (Isa. 55:8-9.)

The Christian accepts gratefully the gift of God in Christ for his salvation, and does not let the mystery dim his faith.

Yet from the standpoint of experience as it is lived, it is not so mysterious. The first Christians had only one creed, "Jesus Christ is Lord." This was enough to make them confront a hostile and skeptical world with their witness, and in persecution to persist steadfastly and go to death singing. This faith is still the mainstay of hosts of lives. The power of Christianity, then and since, has centered in the life, the death, the resurrection, and the living presence of Jesus Christ. Christians have not always maintained the vitality of their faith, but where they have, Christianity has been an incalculable power for good.

Our next theme must be how the Christian church came into being through the power of the Holy Spirit after the death of Jesus. We must also ask what is meant by the church and by the Holy Spirit, and this will lead us into an inquiry about the Christian doctrine of the Trinity.

CHAPTER FIVE

The Holy Spirit and the Church

The Holy Spirit and the church are separate but closely related elements in Christian belief and experience. There are three main reasons why we shall look at them together in this chapter.

An obvious reason is that the church came into existence by the power of the Holy Spirit after the death and resurrection of Jesus. In the experience called Pentecost, at which we shall be looking presently, the Holy Spirit inspired in the early disciples great zeal and fervor and set them to witnessing to their faith. Even to the present, where the church is vital, this witness continues under the leading of the Holy Spirit.

A second reason is that as the church developed through the centuries and changes took place, these steps were usually thought to be prompted by the Holy Spirit and thus to be God's will. In many cases both doctrinal and social factors were involved, but belief in the Holy Spirit as giving divine guidance provided the strongest motivation. Some of these changes were very constructive; others were not so good and therefore presumably were due more to human factors than to the leading of God's Spirit.

A third reason for looking at the church and the Holy Spirit in close conjunction is that through the centuries of Christian history the mainstream of Christianity has believed in the doctrine of the Trinity: that is, in God as Father, Son, and Holy Spirit. The World Council of Churches today accepts for membership only those churches which hold to such a trinitarian position.

Christianity is a thoroughly monotheistic faith. How then can it hold to a doctrine of the Trinity? And what does this mean?

1. *The doctrine of the Trinity.* It is a serious misunderstanding to think of Father, Son, and Holy Spirit as three separate deities. This would be polytheism, not monotheism; it would be tritheism, not the Christian Trinity. It is not surprising that this mistake has been made, for Christians have often spoken of "God in three persons," and one of the great Christian hymns contains the refrain

> Holy, holy, holy, merciful and mighty!
> God in three persons, blessed Trinity!

What the "three persons" meant originally, and what this ought to mean today, is "God in three manifestations," or forms of self-disclosure. What the word "person" in this connection means is suggested by the Latin phrase *dramatis personae,* the characters of a drama; hence, the most accurate understanding might be the "roles" of Father, Son, and Holy Spirit in the great drama of divine revelation and man's salvation.

Thus it is quite possible to think of the one God—the only God—as coming to us in three vital, even indispensable, ways. God the Father is the loving and almighty Creator and Ruler of the universe, who is infinite in wisdom, power, goodness, and love. This God has a yearning love for all men as his children, and is at work everywhere among men for the increase of righteousness, peace, and joy. Because God is our Father, we ought to treat all men as brothers. As we have seen, Jesus throughout his ministry sought to draw men to the worship and service of

God the Father, and it was to this God that he prayed repeatedly and taught his disciples to pray.

God the Son does not mean that Jesus was a second deity. Rather, it means that "God was in Christ," and present in a way that makes it appropriate to speak of him as Lord and Savior. Bearing in mind what was said in the previous chapter about the incarnation, we may appropriately think and speak of him as God incarnate. Though we are all, as God's children, sons and daughters of the Father, only in Jesus are the love and the goodness of God so fully present that we call him the Son of God.

The Word of God, whether this term is applied to the Bible or to Jesus, means God speaking—God disclosing himself. We have noted that in the prologue of John's Gospel Jesus is referred to as the Word that became flesh to dwell among us (John 1:14). A little further along in the same great passage we read: "And from his fullness have we all received, grace upon grace. For the law was given through Moses; grace and truth came through Jesus Christ. No one has ever seen God; the only Son, who is in the bosom of the Father, he has made him known." (John 1:16-18.) The New English Bible significantly translates the last clause, "God's only Son, he who is nearest to the Father's heart, he has made him known." With such overtones it is not difficult to speak of Jesus not only as the Son of God but in a very special sense as God's only Son.

2. *The Holy Spirit.* But what do we mean by the Holy Spirit, the third "person" of the Trinity? Again, we must guard against thinking of a third God. The Holy Spirit is the same God, the infinite and eternal God, acting in our lives, present with us, right here and now. To see what this means we must again turn to the New Testament.

In the account which the author of the fourth Gospel gives us of Jesus' last supper with his disciples, we find him telling them that he must leave them. Yet they would not be left alone, for the Father would send in his name a Counselor, to be with them forever, to lead them to the truth, and help them to remember what he had taught them. (John 14:16-17, 25-26.) As the manifestation of God incarnate in human form, Jesus could be only in one place and for a relatively short time. Therefore he promised, and God gave, another manifestation that could be present in every place and to the end of time. Thus the Holy Spirit may be thought of as the living Christ, not the human Jesus, but the divine Spirit within him that made him God incarnate. This is suggested also in the last words of the Gospel of Matthew, in which after the great commission to go and make disciples of all nations the risen Christ gives the promise, "Lo, I am with you always, to the close of the age" (Matt. 28:20).

God as Father, Son, and Holy Spirit are three disclosures to us of one divinity, and we need all three ways of finding him. This is easier to understand in experience than in the more formal language of theology. It is significant that in the earliest New Testament writings—the letters of Paul—the terms "Holy Spirit," "the Spirit of God," "the Spirit of Jesus Christ," or simply Christ, or the Lord, or the Spirit are used interchangeably and apparently with the same meaning. From his experience as a Christian before any theological doctrine of the Trinity was formulated, Paul found it natural to think of "the Lord" as God the Father, or as Jesus Christ the Son of God, or as the Holy Spirit. And so may we.

This trilogy is suggested by Paul at the end of his second letter to the Corinthians, in which he gives the church his blessing in the words, "The grace of the Lord Jesus Christ and the love of God and the fellowship of the Holy Spirit be with you all" (II Cor. 13:14). These words have been used as a benediction at the close of Christian services of worship for centuries.

3. *What difference does the Holy Spirit make?* The question is sometimes asked as to whether we need the Holy Spirit, when we have the God whom Jesus worshiped and served, with Jesus himself to make him known to us. It may be helpful, therefore, to note what the Holy Spirit does in human life. This is suggested by the words just quoted from the Christian benediction, "the fellowship of the Holy Spirit."

Let us remember that the Holy Spirit means God present with us, God acting for us. Christians believe that God is a majestic Being far above us, and this aspect of God's nature is called the transcendence of God. Yet Christians also believe that God is a loving personal Spirit, concerned about us, very close to us. The belief in the Holy Spirit emphasizes this divine nearness and personal concern, and is the basis of Christian prayer. God as Holy Spirit speaks to us in the deep places of our own spirits, and we can respond to him by our thoughts and lives. We also can speak to him in prayer and feel assured that he hears, and gives to us companionship, guidance, and strength.

The fellowship of the Holy Spirit means, then, companionship in our loneliness. Even when surrounded by people, we find it is not unusual to feel a lack of real companionship and understanding by human friends. A feeling that God is near us, cares about us, and in his infinite wisdom understands us and our human situation makes a great difference in life.

Furthermore, the Holy Spirit gives us guidance, with light upon the decisions we must make. The Holy Spirit will not automatically settle our problems for us, for God expects us to use our minds and the best judgment possible about the situation. Yet the Holy Spirit will help us to discover what Paul called "the mind of Christ," that is, the spirit and attitudes of Jesus. This is suggested in Jesus' promise of the Holy Spirit on the night of the last supper, "But the Counselor, the Holy Spirit, whom the Father will send in my name, he will teach you all things, and bring to your remembrance all that I have said to you" (John 14:26). When the Holy Spirit is listened to and obeyed, we are brought to think and act in a more Christian way, loving, trusting, and serving God, rather than simply following our own selfish desires.

Again, the Holy Spirit supplies strength for daily living. Whether it is in the great crises of life, when sorrow and trouble seem too much to bear in our own human strength, or in the many petty strains that keep us feeling weak and frustrated, the Holy Spirit approached in prayer gives new confidence and strength. The Holy Spirit, coming from God through Christ, forgives the penitent sinner and sets him forward in the way of better and stronger living. What is sometimes called "the witness of the Spirit" gives assurance in the soul that one has been forgiven and accepted by God, and then one can live with an inner peace and a greater strength than would otherwise be possible.

Thus it appears that the Holy Spirit is very important in Christian belief. Because of the Holy Spirit the Christian church came into existence. We must now see how.

4. *Pentecost and the birth of the church.* Although Jesus drew followers about him in his lifetime, there was no real church until after his death and resurrection. Luke, who not only wrote the Gospel that bears his name but the book of Acts, says in the first chapter of Acts that the disciples asked the risen Christ whether the kingdom of God was coming at that time. His answer was, "It is not for you to know times or seasons which the Father has fixed by his own authority. But you shall receive power when the Holy Spirit has come upon you; and you shall be my witnesses in Jerusalem and in all Judea and Samaria and to the end of the earth." (Acts 1:7-8.) The second chapter of Acts tells of the coming of the Holy Spirit soon after, at Pentecost, and of the consequences of this event.

Pentecost was a Jewish holy day, fifty days after the Passover season. The followers of Jesus were together in one place, waiting and receptive, when a great new sense of holy enthusiasm swept over them. As the story has it, "tongues as of fire" rested upon them, and the bystanders heard them speaking, each in his own language. We may perhaps understand this as the glow on their faces, an eagerness to witness for Christ, and a deep unity in Christ which transcended the barriers of race, nation, and language. In any case, after Peter preached a sermon calling them to repentance and offering forgiveness of their sins through Christ, three thousand persons responded. They then shared not only their prayers and their praise to God but their possessions, distributing them to all as any had need. The story of Pentecost ends with the graphic words, "And day by day, attending the temple together and breaking bread in their homes, they partook of food with glad and generous hearts, praising God and having favor with all the people. And the Lord added to their number day by day those who were being saved." (Acts 2:46-47.)

From this time on, the Christian church has been in existence. In the book of Acts and in the letters of the New Testament (those of Paul being written earlier than Acts and several others later) we get glimpses of how the church began to have an organization. There are some descriptions and many occasional hints of the appointment of deacons and bishops as leaders; of how baptism was used as a symbolic rite for the admission into the Christian fellowship of those who became Christians; of the use of bread and wine as a symbolic communal meal in commemoration of Jesus' last supper with his disciples and his death upon the cross for man's salvation. The full elaboration of these sacraments and forms of organization came later, but their beginnings are in the New Testament.

What is very clear from the book of Acts and the letters is the great missionary enthusiasm of the young church. Christians went everywhere, often under great hardship and persecution, telling the "good news" of their faith, for that is what the "gospel" means. Having received the promised power of the Holy Spirit, they took seriously the obligation to be witnesses "in Jerusalem and in all Judea and Samaria and to the end of the earth." As a result, congregations of Christians were formed along the eastern Mediterranean, through Asia Minor, and in southern Europe as far west as Rome. Paul, in particular, was a great missionary as well as theologian and administrator, and it is to the churches he established in his journeys that most of his letters were addressed.

Christians believe that the Holy Spirit did not speak solely in the past, but continues to speak to individual Christians and to churches today, giving guidance and strength as new situations arise. Because of this it is possible not only to look back to the great early days of the church, but to believe that God has been present and acting in its later developments and that he still leads through his Holy Spirit. This is not to say that everything said or done by the churches has always been right, for Christians are human. Yet the revelation of God in Jesus Christ, and the presence of God through the Holy Spirit, are basic to the discovering and the doing of the will of God the Father Almighty, maker of heaven and earth.

5. *What is the Christian church?* Today there are many branches of the Christian church. Some are very large, like the Roman Catholic, the Eastern Orthodox, and numerous Protestant groups. Some are not so large in numbers but are strong in influence and good works, ministering to both the souls and bodies of men. There are some very small churches, often unknown to most of their fellow Christians but certainly not forgotten by God. There are so many branches of the Christian church that we cannot here do more than mention a few of them by name.

There are very old churches that have existed since the early centuries of the Christian era, such as the Coptic in Egypt and the Mar Thoma in India. There are others that have come into existence quite recently. They encircle the earth. There are differences among them which have emerged during the history of the church, but it would require a longer book than this one to describe them. However, the agreements are more important than the differences. Let us take a look at some of these basic agreements.

a. *The church is a fellowship in Christ.* Christianity has never been, and by its very nature it cannot be, a solitary religion. There have been a few Christians—relatively a very few—who have thought they should flee from the world to keep their souls pure. Some persons have been won to Christ by reading the Bible without other human agency. However, the normal way in which Christianity is acquired, experienced, and spread is through groups of Christians in local congregations.

Usually these local congregations are related to larger groups called denominations or communions. We have just now named some of them. They are like families in the larger household of faith. Some of these are very much alike in their beliefs and practices, others differ considerably. Yet all worship God as he comes to us through Christ, and feel their oneness in Christ in spite of the divisions. Of late, two great developments adding to this sense of unity have taken place: (1) most of the Protestant and Eastern Orthodox churches have become associated for fellowship, study, and some forms of action in the World Council of Churches; and (2) the leaders of these groups and of the Roman Catholic Church seem much more willing than formerly to try to understand each other's position.

It is important to stress that a church is a fellowship in Christ. Some local congregations seem to be mainly social fellowships of congenial people, but this is not what a church is intended to be or what it is when the Holy Spirit speaks through it with power.

b. *The church is an institution in society.* While a church is essentially a fellowship in Christ, motivated by the Holy Spirit, it must like any human spirit have a body to function through. Accordingly, the different denominations have forms of government, rules for the selection and ordination of their leaders, boards of management, and agencies for the promotion of the various activities of the churches. These are elements in the society of any place where the churches are located, and the churches must cooperate with or challenge the rest of that society. Sometimes unchristian rivalries or unchristian compromises with the secular culture about them result, but this again is never the church at its best. The true church of Christ puts its loyalty to God above all else, even at the cost of suffering persecution; yet it seeks to witness to its gospel in ways adapted to the needs of the society in which it dwells.

c. *The church proclaims the gospel of Christ.* According to the principles of the Protestant Reformation, the true church is that in which the Word of God is rightly proclaimed and the sacraments rightly administered. The Word, let us remember, means God's disclosure of himself. It means the Bible, but beyond the Bible it means Christ as God's supreme self-disclosure. The proclamation comes through the sermon and the liturgy of the church in its public services of worship, but it comes also through teaching, deeds of Christian service, and in any way in which Christ is made known. In practice, this means that while churches may do and say many of the same things that the other agencies of society do, there ought always to be a Christian center to these activities and forms of expression.

The time-honored definition of a sacrament is "the outward and visible sign of an inward and spiritual grace." These bind Christians around the world together. The two principal Christian sacraments are baptism and the Lord's Supper, or Eucharist.

Baptism signifies entrance by the grace of God into the Christian fellowship, either in infancy through the agency of the Church in conjunction with the vows of the parents, or in adult life through voluntary acceptance of the vows of Christian discipleship. It is done in some churches by immersion, as being the most like the baptism of Jesus; in others, by sprinkling or pouring a little water upon the head of the person being baptized. What gives it special Christian sanctity and meaning along with this act are the words spoken by the minister or priest, "(Name of person), I baptize thee in the name of the Father, and of the Son, and of the Holy Spirit. Amen."

The sacrament of the Lord's Supper, called also Communion or the Eucharist or in Catholic churches the Mass, is the most sacred of all the Christian sacraments. The bread and wine used in it signify the body and the blood of Christ, given upon the cross for man's redemption. It is a holy time of self-examination and penitence before God, rededication to the Christian life, and thanksgiving to God for his grace which comes to men through Christ. It is administered almost always by an ordained priest or minister, and since some churches do not accept the ordination in other churches as valid, problems have arisen as to the conditions under which it may properly be administered or taken. On the whole, however, it is not only a great means of grace to Christians but a deep bond of Christian unity.

d. *The church reaches out to serve the world.* We noted earlier in this chapter how the early church, under the impulse of the Holy Spirit, witnessed to its faith and spread the gospel beyond the Middle East where both Judaism and Christianity were born. This it has continued to do, for Christianity is a missionary religion. There have been times when the churches became somewhat stagnant and seemed to lose their vitality, but when this has happened the Holy Spirit has stirred them again to a new awareness of their message to the world and hence to a new activity and zeal. As a result, Christianity is found today in almost every part of the world, and is still increasing.

The aim of this missionary outreach is not simply to gain numbers of adherents. Christianity is concerned to be of service wherever it goes, whether in lands where it has long been strong or among its younger churches. The churches give pastoral care to the people; they help with good counsel in personal crises and times of trouble, minister in times of joy such as marriage and parenthood, and in times of bereavement and death impart the consolations of Christian faith. Teaching, social work, medical care, literacy, aid to refugees, and other forms of Christian service have been prompted by the Christian duty to love and serve one another. In many cases these services have been taken over by other agencies, but the churches have provided the motive through the Christian desire to be as helpful as possible.

The particular forms such services take vary with the circumstances, as the situation changes and the Holy Spirit leads. Yet always the duty and the privilege of worshiping and serving God, and in response to the call of God serving men in the name and spirit of Christ, remain constant for the churches.

I would like to end this chapter by quoting again Paul's benediction, and saying this as a prayer for every person who may read or hear these words: "May the grace of the Lord Jesus Christ, and the love of God, and the fellowship of the Holy Spirit be with you all. Amen."

CHAPTER SIX

The Christian Life

In this chapter we shall speak of a number of things that give hope to the Christian through trust in God and in the way of life that Christ set before his followers. None of these are identical, though they are all related. This may help to bring together some of the things that have been said in the previous chapters.

1. *Salvation from sin.* Man is a two-sided creature. As we saw in the second chapter, when we thought about God as the Creator, man is made in the spiritual image of God. This means that God has given us great powers—the capacity to think and to work out vast systems of knowledge, the capacity to plan and create and accomplish great exploits, the capacity to love and to encourage harmony and friendship among groups both small and large. These powers all center in that aspect of man's life which distinguishes him most from the animal. This is his freedom, as a morally responsible being, to choose his course of action. This is the main characteristic of the human spirit, and it gives man a dignity and worth which no other creature on earth possesses.

Yet this freedom carries with it great dangers! Because God has made us in his own spiritual image, able to worship, honor, and serve him, we are able also to defy his will. Because we are morally responsible beings and can choose to do good, we can also act irresponsibly and do evil. If we were unable to do otherwise, then the evil would not be our fault. In that case we should be like automatic puppets or machines, with which one might get out of patience if something went wrong but which could not be charged with sinning. Because God in his wisdom and great goodness has made us not puppets or machines but free, responsible human spirits, we are able to disobey him and fall into sin. This we do—every one of us.

Sin is rebellion against God. We can speak both of *sin* as a persistent state of the soul when one insists on having his own way in defiance of God, and of *sins* as particular acts or attitudes of wrongdoing. As for these sins, which take many forms, there is no special list by which to check one's self as having committed many or few, great or small ones, and feel self-righteous if the record looks good! They center in violations of the love commandments of Jesus, "You shall love the Lord your God with all your heart, and with all your soul, and with all your mind, and with all your strength," and, "You shall love your neighbor as yourself" (Mark 12:30, 31). The Roman Catholic Church has long had a list of seven "deadly" sins —pride, anger, envy, avarice, sloth, gluttony, and lust. These are certainly sins, and foes of right living in the sight of God, but it is doubtful that all the many unloving things we feel and do can be brought within this list.

More persistent and intangible than any particular act of wrongdoing is sin as a state of the soul. This roots in our self-will, our indifference to God and his will, our self-righteous attempts to run our own lives in defiance of God and, quite often, in defiance of the feelings and needs of other people.

God loves even the worst sinner, but he hates sin. Because of our sin, we all stand under the judgment of the righteous God. It will not do to think of the love of God as any light or sentimental overlooking of human sin. Sin is the world's most serious kind of evil.

If this were the whole situation, there would not be much

hope for us. Paul describes very vividly the plight of the person who wants to stop sinning but finds temptation too strong for him: "For though the will to do good is there, the deed is not. The good which I want to do, I fail to do; but what I do is the wrong which is against my will; and if what I do is against my will, clearly it is no longer I who am the agent, but sin that has its lodging in me." (Rom. 7:18-20 NEB.)

If we are honest with ourselves, have we not all felt like that sometimes? We might also say in despair, as Paul does a little further on, "Miserable creature that I am, who is there to rescue me out of this body doomed to death?" (Rom. 7:24 NEB.)

The answer came to Paul on the Damascus road when he heard Jesus Christ speak to him, and he became a new man. No wonder, then, that he answers this question with a joyous, triumphant exclamation, "God alone, through Jesus Christ our Lord! Thanks be to God! . . . There is no condemnation for those who are united with Christ Jesus, because in Christ Jesus the life-giving law of the Spirit has set you free from the law of sin and death." (Rom. 7:25-8:2 NEB.)

This sense of release and victory over sin has been the experience of Christians for many centuries. It does not come to everybody in just the same way. Since the time of Paul many others have had a conversion experience as sudden and dramatic as his. But not all do. For those who have been connected with a Christian church and have had Christian teaching and influences from their childhood, the process of becoming a Christian is usually a more gradual one. Yet it is as real, and where Christianity is vital, it is as joyous and life transforming.

So the primary, great note in Christian experience is God's forgiveness of the repentant sinner and his gift of new life through Christ. This does not mean that one is no longer tempted, or that he never sins again. This would make life too easy! We must still exercise our responsible freedom of choice in life's decisions. Yet the Holy Spirit stands ready to give us companionship, guidance, and strength. We can go forward without fear, knowing that God is with us.

2. *Mastery over pain.* There is a second form of evil from which everybody naturally desires to be delivered, whether he is a Buddhist, Hindu, Muslim, or has no religion at all. This is suffering.

Yet nobody *can* be completely delivered from it. Most people do not suffer physical pain all the time, and much has been done to relieve bodily illness. More can be done, and ought to be done both out of a humanitarian concern for persons and out of response to the Christian love commandment. Yet few persons grow to maturity without suffering some physical pain, and some persons suffer a great deal. Then old age brings on still more infirmities.

Even if one is largely spared physical pain, there is a great range of mental pain—disappointment, discouragement, frustration, a sense of inferiority and distrust of one's ability to cope with life, distrust of others, resentment at being unjustly treated and sometimes even persecuted, often a sense of being rejected, unloved, and unwanted. Also, if one has a sensitive conscience there is likely to be a haunting sense of guilt from the realization of having done wrong. Add to these the anxieties that come in every person's life and the inevitable grief that comes with the loss of loved ones, and life at times becomes very hard to bear.

What has Christian faith to offer in such a situation? We shall look first at physical suffering, though the two kinds are rather closely connected.

Some Christians believe that bodily ailments can be healed through faith; others are more doubtful. It is certainly recorded in the Bible that Jesus healed both physical and mental forms of illness. Numerous miracles of healing have been reported all down through the history of the church, and still are. Some of these were doubtless real and permanent, whereas in other cases the malady returned after the fervor of the experience wore off.

There is now a much better understanding than formerly about the close connection between bodily and mental states. When a person is worried, or angry, or deeply unhappy, or in nervous tension for any other reason, it is apt to affect his health. Restore his peace of mind and his bodily pains recede. The serenity and strength of character that come from trust in God can help to reduce or banish physical pain. However, most Christians believe that God expects us to use the best possible hygiene, sanitation, and medical care, and that to make these available to others is a Christian duty. It is not in faith and prayer alone, but in such services along with the spiritual fruits of prayer, that our best hope lies.

In the matter of mental pain, religion and self-understanding must work together. Unhappiness has so many sources that it is important to look at one's self objectively, and this a counselor can often help one do. If the counselor is a person of Christian faith, he will not hesitate to show the relevance of faith to many of these sources of disturbance. If the unhappiness is due to a sense of guilt, even though a latent and subconscious one, confession and repentance with the knowledge of God's forgiveness will take the burden away and help one to make a new start. When the sin has been against another person, acknowledgment in penitence and making amends as far as possible for the injury will help to restore the broken relationship. When the cause of our mental pain is petty selfishness or self-pity with the expectation that the world ought to give us what we want, the Christian faith will broaden our horizons. When a real injury has been done us, God will help us to forgive. When there is some deeper cause of distress that cannot be avoided or corrected, God will help us to endure it triumphantly.

But how is God related to the suffering in the world? Why does he let it happen?

Sin is always evil in the sight of God, and ought to be regarded as the worst evil by men. Pain is not always an evil. It gives us danger signals of things that ought to be corrected, as in bodily pain that tells us we need a doctor. Some pain is good for us, to promote growth in strength of character. A child or an adult who always has his own way and who cares about nothing but pleasure is seldom a strong or admirable character. With a wisdom greater than that of any human parent, God the Father of us all provides some pain for the discipline and strengthening of personality. Though we shrink from it when it comes, it is not unusual in looking back to see that good has come from it.

Christians believe that we ought to accept the will of God in confident trust of his goodness. Nevertheless, Christians believe that there is more pain in human life than God desires men to suffer, and hence that not all of it *is* the will of God. When it is due to causes that are clearly the fault of man, or to causes that could be eliminated by intelligent human action if men cared enough, then it is hardly proper to call it the will of God.

Not all of human suffering comes from human sin, though much of it does, and this God certainly wants us to conquer by his help. Some of it comes from our being so closely related to one another in the family, or the nation, or the human race—a blessing we pervert when hatred or rivalry or some other form of injury replaces the helpfulness and harmony of spirit that God wills. Some comes from natural forces in the kind of world God has given us in order that we might live securely in a world of dependable order and natural law. These forces we must learn to understand, to master, to live with, and to use in God's service as his responsible stewards. The injunction to "subdue the earth" found in the first chapter of Genesis still holds today.

In regard to pain Christian belief takes two important forms. One of these is the obligation to obey the love commandment of Jesus by feeling compassion for those who suffer, relieving pain that can be prevented or lessened. Now that so much is known of the causes of both physical and mental pain, this would mean learning all we can and acting accordingly. The second great Christian conviction is that God, if we seek his help with sincerity and trust, will help us to endure and to triumph over whatever afflictions may assail us. "We know that in everything God works for good with those who love him" (Rom. 8:28), and in his presence and power we can go forward to finer, stronger living.

This brings us to the deepest note in the mastery of pain. Jesus went to the cross although his agony in Gethsemane tells us clearly that he did not want to die. Yet he did what God called him to do out of love for men. For us today, the way of the cross means incurring pain willingly when duty to God or love for other persons requires it. There is no virtue in suffering simply to make a display of martyrdom, or to receive pity. That would be a subtle and unlovely form of self-centeredness. Yet there are times when following the love commandment leads us into suffering that could be avoided if we were less faithful. Sometimes today witness and fidelity mean dying for our faith, but more often they mean unkind criticism and social disapproval, or the loss of one's job or opportunities for advancement.

All this takes stamina, and in our own strength we quail before it, taking the easier and "safer" course of doing or saying nothing. This happens so often that it is the chief barrier to the church's influence in society. Yet as Christians we can take the way of the cross when we know that Jesus has led the way and that the Holy Spirit is with us. This occurred again and again in the early days of the Christian church; it has occurred throughout the centuries since; it occurs today where Christianity is vital and faithful to its Lord.

Once more we find from Paul some of the greatest words ever written about the mastery of pain. These words stand at the end of the same chapter of his letter to the Romans from which were quoted the opening words about the conquest of sin through Christ.

> Who shall separate us from the love of Christ? Shall tribulation, or distress, or persecution, or famine, or nakedness, or peril, or sword? . . . No, in all these things we are more than conquerors through him who loved us. For I am sure that neither death, nor life, nor angels, nor principalities, nor things present, nor things to come, nor powers, nor height, nor depth, nor anything else in all creation, will

be able to separate us from the love of God in Christ Jesus our Lord. (Rom. 8:35-39.)

3. *Life after death.* All persons tend to shrink from pain. Sin ought to be the concern of all, though we are usually too complacent about it. Yet neither sin nor pain is the most intractable foe of the human spirit. "The last enemy to be destroyed," says Paul in another letter, "is death." (I Cor. 15:26.) All men must die, and while the coming of death may be delayed, there is nothing in the end that we can do about it.

The attitudes about death in current society vary greatly. They range from dread and terror, through acceptance of its inevitability as an unpleasant necessity, to a sense of the meaninglessness of life which prompts people to commit suicide. Loneliness, frustration, anxiety, and the various causes of mental pain listed in the previous section are often the cause of this last attitude, especially when one has neither human companionship nor a sustaining faith in God.

There are many persons who do not believe that there is any life after death, dismissing this as an outgrown superstition. Some say that they would not want to live on if they could, though these same persons usually feel keenly the separation when death takes away those they love. On the whole, one may say that belief in, and hope of, eternal life has faded considerably within the past century, as more emphasis than formerly is being given to the body with its brain and nerve cells as the source of human personality.

In the Christian church also there have been changes, though not of the same kind. Formerly, there was a very strong emphasis on the hope of reward in heaven and the fear of divine punishment in hell. With this was linked the idea that "being saved" meant being sure of going to heaven at death and avoiding hell, and not much attention was given to the quality of the present life. This still persists enough so that it has seemed wise to emphasize in this book that salvation through Christ makes a great difference in the world where we now live.

Yet it would be a serious mistake to leave the impression that Christians are so concerned with the present life as to be unconcerned about the vista of eternity beyond death. The mainstream of Christian belief affirms the existence of eternal life as the gift of God and also the reality of divine judgment. This belief in an eternal life of blessedness beyond the pains and sorrows and struggles of the present world is our ultimate Christian hope.

Most Christians do not try to locate heaven in astronomical space or to describe pictorially its nature. It is recognized that such phrases in the Bible as Jesus' reference to "many mansions," and the jewelled walls, pearly gates, and golden streets of the book of Revelation are symbolic rather than literal descriptions of that which is beyond our sense-bound human imagination. Nevertheless, though most Christians are reluctant to claim to know more than we do, there are great assurances in the Christian hope of life after death. What then can we feel sure of?

First, eternal life is given to us by the goodness and power of God; it is not something to claim as a natural right or earn by our merit. The same God who brought Jesus from the realm of death, victorious over sin and death, can give us eternal life also if it is his will and purpose. It is not something that is likely to be proved or disproved scientifically, for it lies outside the realm of scientific observation; but it is something to be accepted by faith as appropriate to the nature of God and promised by Christ.

In the second place, though we do not earn our immortality by our own effort, the decisions we make and the lives we lead here have a definite relation to it. There is continuity between this life and the next, even though these bodies die and disintegrate in the elements. Paul speaks of a "spiritual body" which God will give us in the next life. (I Cor. 15:40, 44.) Just what this is we do not know, but Paul's analogy of a grain of wheat that falls to the ground and dies that new life may come from it is a helpful one. And if there is such continuity of personality in the spiritual sense, it is vitally important that we make the right decisions, living the saved life here, if this is to go on into eternity.

In the Christian sense the saved life, whether for this world or for eternity, means companionship with Christ—God's nearer presence as we seek in the light of his Spirit to do his will. The opposite—alienation or separation from God through our own self-will—incurs divine judgment. In blunt terms, it means hell. There is reason to believe that this, too, continues after death and marks the plight of him who willfully refuses to respond to the love of God.

The future life for those who make the response of faith and love may be looked forward to without anxiety and with peace of mind and soul. One does not then hasten toward death, but accepts it when it comes as part of the good providence of God. So, too, when the death of a loved one occurs, one may know that he is safe in the hands of a loving and just God, and when death claims us also there can be a glad reunion in a realm beyond earthly sorrows. There is symbolism, but also deep truth, in the words used by the author of the book of Revelation to describe what lies beyond this earthly realm of sin and pain:

> Behold, the dwelling of God is with men. He will dwell with them, and they shall be his people, and God himself will be with them; he will wipe away every tear from their eyes, and death shall be no more, neither shall there be mourning nor crying nor pain any more, for the former things have passed away. (Rev. 21:3-4.)

These words describe what the author saw as the situation when the kingdom of God should have fully come; they apply equally to the individual Christian's hope of eternal life.

What, then, is the ultimate Christian hope? It is the hope that to life lived in the presence of God, death is but the entrance into a larger life. It is the hope that in the larger fellowship of God's sons for time and eternity there is no final separation from those we love. It is the hope that whether death comes early or late, no life is fruitless, no personality prized by God as an infinitely precious creation will go out like a candle in the dark.

Furthermore, this hope has its bearing on society as well. We ought to do everything possible on earth to make this a better world, a sphere of greater harmony and good will. Yet if atomic or chemical or bacteriological warfare, or an intercontinental ballistic missile bearing a hydrogen bomb, should cause life upon this planet to end in mutual destruction, life would still go on by the power and the goodness of God in his eternal kingdom. This is no warrant for complacency or a cessation of human effort for peace; it is the assurance that God reigns in a realm that is beyond the power of men to destroy.

So, in whatever manner death comes to us, the Christian who trusts the providence of God need have no personal fear of it, though he ought to do all that he can to avert it for those about him. There is much more that we should like to know about the nature of the life beyond death, but God in Christ has taught us all that we really need to know.

The Christian believes that Jesus rose triumphant over death on the first Easter morning, and therefore he finds great meaning in the promise of Jesus to his disciples on the night of the last supper, "Because I live, you shall live also." Add to this the continuing assurance of the Holy Spirit, and faith becomes securely grounded without need of further evidence. "'Things beyond our seeing, things beyond our hearing, things beyond our imagining, all prepared by God for those who love him,' these it is that God has revealed to us through the Spirit." (I Cor. 2:9-10 NEB.)

That there is much in our time that is uncertain, no one can deny. Not even the wisest of human persons, whether statesman or common citizen, knows how all the tensions of our time are going to be resolved. Yet among the vicissitudes and anxieties of the earthly scene, of this we can be confident, that if we put our trust in God, the Lord of time and eternity will guide and guard us still.

CPSIA information can be obtained
at www.ICGtesting.com
Printed in the USA
LVHW100413100322
713106LV00020B/299